LEAD YOUR MIND TO LEAD THE WORLD

LEAD YOUR MIND TO LEAD THE WORLD

V. S. GOPALAKRISHNA

GOOD TIMES BOOKS PVT. LTD.
New Delhi (India)
www.goodtimesbooks.com

Published by

Good Times Books Pvt. Ltd.

H-13, Bali Nagar, New Delhi-110 015 (INDIA)

Phones: +91-11-25913301, 45069086 *Fax:* +91-11-45069086

Email : info@goodtimesbooks.com

Website : www.goodtimesbooks.com

First Published 2011

ISBN-13 : 978-93-806193-1-6

Cataloging in Publication Data--DK

Courtesy: D.K. Agencies (P) Ltd.

<docinfo@dkagencies.com>

Gopalakrishna, V. S.

Lead your mind to lead the world / V.S. Gopalakrishna.

p. cm.

ISBN 9789380619316

1. Management--Moral and ethical aspects--India. 2. Management--Moral and ethical aspects. 3. Leadership--Moral and ethical aspects--India. 4. Leadership--Moral and ethical aspects. I. Title.

DDC 658.400954 23

Printed in India at

Salasar Imaging Systems

Dedicated to

RISHIS & ACHARYAS

My Parents V.N.SRINIVASAN & RAJALAKSHMI

My Wife MALATHY *&* *My Son* ADITYA

CONTENTS

YOUR THOUGHTS

become

WORDS

become

ACTION

become

HABITS

become

CHARACTER

become

DESTINY

FOREWORD

The book *Lead your Mind to Lead the World* is good food for thought for CEOs and Senior Managers. This book emphasises the importance of using the spiritual quotient to handle the daily ups and downs of any business scenario. It is seldom used but whoever has used it in the past has benefited as it gives a totally different angle to look at issues or crisis situations.

Lots of references have been drawn from various ancient manuscripts to kindle the thought process. The answers to all the problems that exist have been solved in the past by great thinkers without much theoretical management degrees and *gyan*.

This has been possible as intelligence with spiritual quotient provides the best solution to every problem.

By far there are very few authors who have thought on these lines in the current century at least.

If not one of the best it still has a lot to offer managers to manage their lives and business well.

Lead your Mind to Lead the World

I recommend this book to everyone who aspires to be a great business leader in the future.

P.T.Venkatesh
Commercial Director
HITS Information Technology
William Hare Group, London

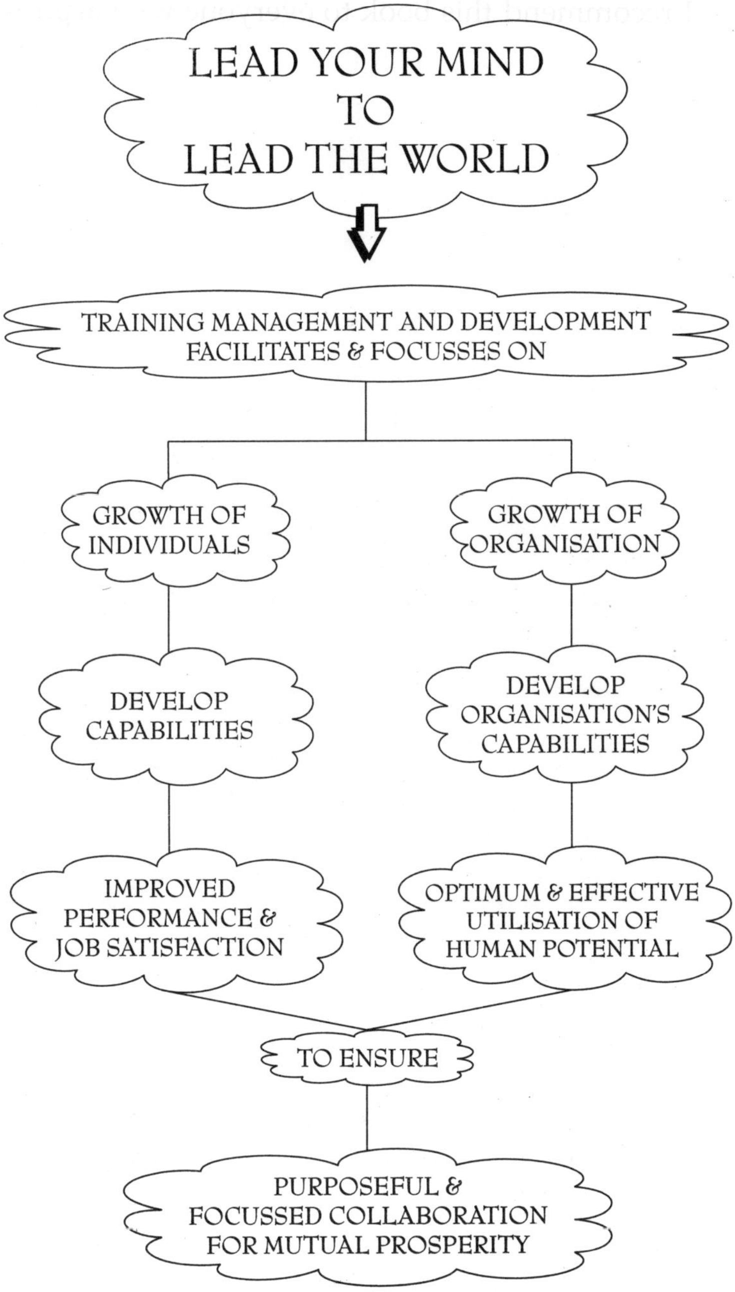
LEAD YOUR MIND
TO
LEAD THE WORLD
TRAINING MANAGEMENT AND DEVELOPMENT
FACILITATES & FOCUSSES ON
GROWTH OF
INDIVIDUALS
GROWTH OF
ORGANISATION
DEVELOP
CAPABILITIES
DEVELOP
ORGANISATION'S
CAPABILITIES
IMPROVED
PERFORMANCE &
JOB SATISFACTION
OPTIMUM & EFFECTIVE
UTILISATION OF
HUMAN POTENTIAL
TO ENSURE
PURPOSEFUL &
FOCUSSED COLLABORATION
FOR MUTUAL PROSPERITY

PART-I

THE SPIRITUAL POWER

Four Steps of Great Life

1. Look Back and Thank God.
2. Look Forward and Trust God.
3. Look Around and Believe God.
4. Look Within Yourself and Find God.

–Anonymous

1

THE SPIRITUAL QUOTIENT

From IQ to EQ, we have travelled this far. The new buzzword most of the organizations are speaking about now is SQ- Spiritual Quotient.

Let us see what SQ is all about:

In today's fast-changing world, materialism and stress have become part of our everyday lives. We are constantly looking for answers: How can one live a successful and happy life?

One way of finding answers to this question could be to explore the Spiritual Quotient (SQ), relating to our ability to understand and comprehend the spiritual aspects of life, which, contrary to popular belief, are not necessarily connected to religion.

Most of us are familiar with the concept of the Intelligence Quotient (IQ).

In the mid '90s, Daniel Goleman started talking

about EQ or Emotional Quotient. Danah Zoher and Ian Marshal in their recent work *SQ: Connecting with our Spiritual Intelligence* observe "While computers have IQ and animals can have EQ, it is essentially an SQ that sets human beings apart." Therefore, for the 'Wheel of Life' to roll smoothly, all the spokes of the wheel - IQ, EQ and SQ - have to be equally developed. The journey from IQ to SQ represents moving from the gross to the subtle, finite to infinite and from tangible to intangible.

SQ has several dimensions: Compassion, wholeness, self-esteem, gratitude, spirit of surrender and service and the ego. Handling the ego is one of the critical dimensions of enhancing the SQ. Ego issues, if not handled with care, can create problems in our personal, social and professional lives. Hence for better relationships, it is very important to understand and handle the ego — both of the 'self' and others.

Ego stems from our bundle of memories. It is further reinforced when we repeatedly embrace a particular thought for extended periods. We tend to take 'ego positions' based on what happened to us in the past. One of the key aspects of handling the ego is to analyse the way in which our thoughts are organized because our ego is embedded deep into our thought process.

Our thoughts are often organized in a hierarchical order. First, there is a primary layer of thought, which constitutes the core, and then there is a second layer, a third layer, and so on. The primary layer represents objectivity of thoughts and maturity whereas the subsequent layers represent subjective interpretations often arising out of perceptions which may be far from reality.

Shri Ramana Maharishi advised that one should contemplate primarily on the inner core rather than on the secondary and tertiary layers; for once we concentrate on the core thoughts, we will naturally look at the events of life more objectively. Once we are objective and deal with issues with all gentleness, care and with a *satvik* approach, all our transactions become free from the ego.

J Krishnamurthy calls this state of mind as one of "All Conclusive Awareness." Staying in this state softens our ego. To handle the ego, one has to therefore promote objectivity, for, with objectivity comes truth. This in turn dilutes the ego. Once our actions originate from the depth of our heart representing the primary layer, the path for ego-free relationships will be paved.

Dealing with the ego becomes easier if we can instil a spirit of 'surrender' in our psyche. The environment around you becomes tranquil and peaceful. Surrendering essentially means crucifixion of our ego, but surrendering becomes a rather difficult and painful process because of our worldly attachments.

Krishna in the Bhagavat Gita (chapter 1) says: "Fly unto Him for refuge with all your being, O Bharata; by His grace you shall obtain supreme peace and eternal abode". Krishna advises Arjuna to surrender his ego unto Him.

Commenting on this, Swami Chinmayananda says that "The surrender unto the Lord should not be a temporary self deception; it should be done with a total spirit of devotion and with a state of ego-lessness." This was the spirit exhibited by Radha, Prahlada and Hanuman.

Surrendering the ego is often construed as a weakness. On the contrary, the spirit of surrender enhances our quality of goodness, which ultimately leads to godliness. However, where is God? Vedanta says He resides within us.

By surrendering the ego, we will be able to perpetually experience Spiritual Actualization, leading to a higher SQ. For, "We are not human beings having spiritual experience, but spiritual beings having human experience."

Eight Signs of High SQ

(i) Flexibility

(ii) Self-awareness

(iii) Ability to face and use suffering

(iv) The ability to be inspired by a vision

(v) An ability to see connections between diverse things (thinking holistically)

(vi) A desire and capacity to cause as little harm as possible

(vii) A tendency to probe and ask fundamental questions

(viii) An ability to work against convention

Our lives are not determined by what happens to us but by how we react to what happens. Not by what life brings to us, but by the attitude we bring to life. A positive attitude causes a chain reaction of positive thoughts, events and outcomes. It is a catalyst, a spark that creates extraordinary results.

Let's change to make a change!!!

"If you focus on results, you will never change.

If you focus on change, you will get results"

There Is A Better Way For Everything.
Find it.

–Anonymous

2

ART AND SCIENCE OF INSPIRED LIVING

Purusha means human beings, either a male human being or a female human being. *Artha* means wealth, goal, effort or a destination.

Purushartha means that which is sought after by every human being. It also means freewill, choice, effort, or endeavour. The primary meaning is human destination or human goal. Only human beings seek these goals, not animals or plants. We all know very well that life is by choice and not by chance. No doubt human beings are similar to animals and plants but one common feature that distinguishes them from animals and plants is the use of the intellect, power of reasoning, rational or thinking faculty. All living beings seek food, and after any activity, all take rest. Some animals sleep standing as some human beings also sleep standing while commuting in a bus or train. Some people sleep lying down and some sleep sitting.

Therefore, the similarity is great between human beings, plants and animals. The next one is fear of the external world. A feeling of insecurity and therefore an attempt to protect itself from fear. Then the next one is propagation of one's own species through children, grand children, great grand children and *parampara* etc. These four are common to plants, animals and human beings. However, if all are the same why do we consider human beings superior to other species? Rare is human birth, why do we say this? Because intellect, thinking faculty, judging faculty, reasoning faculty, projecting the future faculty, foresightedness, planning for the future and working for betterment of the future— all these come under intellect or rational faculty.

Since *buddhi* alone makes a human being superior, if we do not have intellect or if we do not use the intellect, we are as good or as bad as animals.

There are some philosophers who advise: don't use your intellect or never use your intellect which is the cause of all human problems, and therefore their teaching is: don't use your intellect. What an unfortunate piece of advice! In addition, the *sastras* say if the intellect is not used human beings are as good or as bad as animals only. Therefore, use your intellect. It is a unique faculty available only to us. Because of this extra faculty we are also extremely self-conscious, capable of self-judgment and capable of comparing ourselves with other human beings which animals or plants do not have .When there is a dog show they have a competition to find out which dog is best trained. Dogs are asked to do various things, then they are given gold, silver and bronze medals and there may be three victory stands also like in the Olympics. When the dogs are on these three stands, what are the feelings they have? "I have gold. I have bronze or silver, I missed gold by 100th of a second". No, dogs do not have inferiority or superiority complexes. They only put their tongues out and look here and there. They do not know what the hell or heaven is happening. On the other hand, the owner of the dog has an inferiority or superiority complex. Therefore, intellect gives one a unique faculty of self-judgment, complex development, and comparison with other members etc. We certainly think of improving our selves in the future and therefore planning becomes another natural consequence of the rational faculty. We also try to project our future hoping that we will be better off. And for improvement of the future, we start planning and the planning is divided into several levels of immediate goals, short term goals or long term goals etc. In the first year we expect one crore business. The next year we expect five crores business. In the fifth year we expect and want our organization to grow to the level of hundred crores profit and so on. Therefore, we have a lot of secondary and primary goals, which we alone are capable of having. Interview the dog, which has got the second prize, and ask it if at the next dog show it wants to come first. What will the dog do! It will put its tongue out and bark. It does not have a plan for the next dog show. So all animals and plants have an instinctive life style. Their entire life is governed by instincts, whereas human beings are governed by instincts also because it is common to animals and plants but more than instincts they are governed by the Intellect. Human beings predominantly have the capacity to discriminate and can choose their future. In addition, because of this choice, human beings entertain a number of goals and all these goals are called *purusharthas.* Now the next question is: how many such goals are possible. If you start enumerating the goals, intermediary and ultimate, short-term, long term, they are countless. However, even though goals are endless we classify them into four categories. Any goal, which you try to accomplish, will come under these four categories. There is no fifth variety. The first one starts very early in life. It is the goal of survival or security. Every-thing that you procure for the sake of security and all those things will come under the first category. In addition, there are food, clothing, shelter, and health. I hope you would have seen the film *Roti, Kapada aur Makan.* In addition, by security I mean sheer physical survival. Right from birth one instinctive and natural urge every living being has is the urge to survive somehow. Anything that you procure for your security i.e. all those objects which contribute to your security, will come under the first category. Physical survival will help you in discarding your sense of insecurity. These objects are

1. Food: Right from the beginning the struggle begins.
2. Clothing to protect our body from the environment.

The types of clothing we have are summer clothing, winter clothing, or nightdress and so on.

Books are written on clothing alone. Special magazines are dedicated for clothing only. The helmet you wear for security or the seat belt you wear in the car for your security and the breathing filter. Have you seen some people wearing a breathing filter while driving a bike? We do not know who is a terrorist and who is not. They tie a kerchief over their mouth. These are all meant for security. In addition, you air-condition your office, home, or car so that pollution in the city will not affect you. Anything that heals our body that is food, clothing, shelter, etc. comes under the first category. Some animals come with natural designer clothing i.e. they do not need clothes as they are gifted with thick and designer skins. Then comes shelter, we are working for a home. We at least want a flat or a small place in a coastal area as our home. Before one dies everyone wants to own a house or at least a flat in a city, village or out of the city. Then comes health, fighting all forms of diseases. The question is should you work hard or work smart," YES" say the *Sastras.* Whether we are useful to society or to ourselves, we have to work hard and be smart. Because we want to live or survive or exist. Initially we want to take care of our own security, then comes the second layer of security that is the security for our future. Because of old age, we cannot work or we cannot earn. In the olden days, the thought was that children would take care of the security of parents in old age. Now-a-days there is a doubt whether the children will take care of us or we have to take care of them. In addition, some tell me, they have confidence in their children but they do not know what type of daughter-in-law or son-in-law they will get. Whether they will allow them to take care of their parents is a big question.

A big question is inside the black box.

I had better save for my future food, future clothing, future shelter and future health etc. and fear of health or diseases grows more and more as we grow older. In the initial part of life food and clothing become important and in the later part of life shelter and health become important. Therefore, we visualize the possible troubles. Next, we are worried about unexpected accidental threats and therefore we have to take all forms of insurance. Health insurance, life insurance, home insurance, theft, earthquake and even tsunami insurance etc. So present security, future security and then comes the next layer of security. Once we possess a few things or people for our security we are worried again about their security. This is how it spreads into a big Ramayana, doesn't it? Security, security for security, etc. First, we want clothes for our body, now we regularly have to wash then in a washing machine for the security of our clothes. I also know there are human washing machines where you just have to lie down in the bathtub; the rest is taken care of. We have to just scrub our body with soap, as simple as that isn't it? Then there is a power fluctuation so we buy a stabilizer for our washing machine for its security. Our house gives us security but we are worried about the security of our house. Therefore, we employ a security guard and we feel insecure if the security guard of the building or house is on leave. Since our security is very important for the security of the house, we have a replacement security for the security. Some tell me they are safe only if he comes. Thus, most of our life we are busy providing for security and all these things come under the first category : freedom from fear of physical survival. In addition, some say they have money for generations and own a reasonable house with their own earnings and now the question is what else to do with life. When all these have been taken care of we go to the second category called comforts or entertainment. These comforts are not required for our security but if we can enjoy them or have all forms of entertainment, we think we have bliss. Therefore, all entertainment comes in the second variety. We want to enjoy ourselves in the form of music, in the form of dance or drama or TV. Some want cable connections and some other connections also. In addition, we know the entertainment industry is so big. We want to go to five star or seven star hotels, beach holiday resorts, hill stations and on a small world tour. What do you mean by small world tour? Yes, we try to restore our mind from the stress and strain of life. Once I take care of entertainment within my surroundings I am bored. I move to other places, a big universal tour to see places and try to admire their culture, learn about them, and adapt to the conditions and life styles of the USA, Japan, China, Europe, South Africa and so on. Therefore, we want to visit all developed, developing, and backward nations or at least visit the USA once. Animals also want comfort, enjoyment and entertainment but they get it instinctively whereas we plan for it. If there is a lot of sun animals naturally go towards the shade, whereas we enter our office cabin and switch on our A/C. Sometimes in the afternoon while at work on a summer day, we come home and relax in air conditioned comfort. Therefore, human beings plan and entertain themselves. In addition, in many countries people do not cross the first state or category. In addition, in some developed countries people start their life in excitement and comfort.

The third category is known as an invisible form of wealth, which we generally translate in English as good luck or good fortune. We say that a person is very lucky, he has good fortune. He was lucky, or I was fortunate. Therefore, we translate this as that which brings us security, comfort and excitement or wealth. That is why in Tamil we call it *adirshtam*. *Koun banega crore pathi?* No doubt, a lot of knowledge and skill is required to enter the contest and in Star TV or Sun TV or the stock market to become a *crorepati,* people call you lucky or fortunate. These are invisible forms of wealth, which they attribute to good luck. Good luck is something which also contributes to our next birth. In the initial stages of life if you study any human birth, our initial few years of life happen to us without our control. They do not come consulting with us but come due to our past good *karma*. What type of parents we have is determined and we find ourselves helpless. We may wish our parents were a little rich or if one would have been born to J.R.D. Tata or the Birlas but these are determined by God and not by us. It is determined by our own choice or freewill that we exerted in our previous births that has determined our present birth. They determine your future existence whether good or bad. I have no choice of my past but I have a choice of my current birth. Hence, life is by choice and not by chance as many think. Good luck has no role to play a part in life but we describe it in such a manner. Sometimes we are born as orphans or with good parents and a different environment, may be in Nigeria! We may be a child doted upon or a beaten child. But we can control or choose our future life. So I feel even though I am a human being my initial few years are not under my control. Then under whose control are they? They are supposed to be determined by freewill or choice of my past birth. My *dharma* will not only help me in this life but also in the next life in providing a good childhood, good food, good environment, good clothing, good parents, good shelter and good values also.

Therefore, a child's life is determined by an invisible form of wealth called good luck. Today psychologists are discovering more and more and they are saying many of our emotional conditions during our adulthood are acquired from our childhood. Therefore, our childhood heavily determines our physical health, mental health, and even future health and therefore if you want to control your childhood it can be done through *dharma purushartha,* free will, choice or effort now. The law of Karma directly influences my past life, present life, future life. Now tell me where is the problem? In fact, we are the problem and we are the solution. In life, all situations and incidents are only 10 percent and the remaining 90 percent is how we respond to those situations. How we handle our situations, goals, choice, or human effort. We not only talk about visible wealth but also try to acquire an invisible form of wealth called good luck or *punya* or subtle form of wealth. These three human goals have many things in common and since they are common, together they are known as *dharma* + *artha* + *kama* = *preyaha* which means all human goals and endeavour. Now the question is what is the fourth or last goal? The fourth human goal is called *moksha* or *mukthi*. *Moksha* means freedom. Freedom from what? Is it political freedom, economic freedom, or spiritual freedom? It is an inner freedom. It is freedom from bondage or attachment. Freedom from slavery with regard to all the above three categories of human goals mentioned earlier. It is freedom from all other accomplishments. In what way am I slave to anything in this world? Any object in the world or anything or person enslaves me in two ways: one by its very absence; second by its very presence. Therefore things bind me by their presence and things strain me by their absence creating a vacuum. Some objects or people create problems by their presence and some by their absence and some create by both presence and absence. Take the case of money, poverty is a problem and prosperity is also a problem. Some go to ashrams because of poverty and some because of prosperity to seek peace of mind. Slavery with regard to external goals is bondage. Freedom from this slavery is otherwise called self-mastery, I am no more a slave, I am a *sant*. Please do not think if you wear an orange dress, you are a *sant* or God. An external *sant* will also say he does not have enough followers. He has attachment towards the act of having lots of disciples. He also thinks he has no ashram of his own or institution in the name of charity. Then some people say they have done so many things but they do not have disciples or they do not have readership of their books and teachings or no circulation of their books. No business with profit? Some say even if people read their books they do not follow them some say they have no followers so they are unhappy. What a great joke? They say they miss name and fame and power. *Swamithwam* is an internal condition not an external one. That is, when things are absent there is no vacuum and when they are present one is not a slave nor are they a burden. I buy a shoe to protect my feet from thorns or stones but now the shoe is not fitting properly and it bites, therefore I am disturbed by the very presence of the shoe. Similarly our life has to be holistic. When I have a shoe, I am burdened and when I had naked feet and legs, I was unhappy. In fact, we are worried or we do not know how to handle most problems as well as the presence of problems themselves. Therefore, internal freedom is a comfortable position with or without objects, people, or anything. It means I must be comfortable with all objects and persons. This inner mastery is *moksha* or inner strength; inner mastery or internal mastery is called freedom from bondage, *moksha,* or *mukthi* in life. Ninety percent of our time is spent responding to 10 percent of incidents so if you know how to handle objects, people and situations you are a master. The first three are secondary goals and the primary goal is the last one—freedom from bondage with respect to the goals. People I come across generally ask me who my role model is. Whoever be my role model, I have to understand that I have some role to play in this life.

The roles are of

1. A child
2. A student
3. A husband/ wife
4. A father/ mother
5. A relative
6. A manager or executive
7. A responsible citizen
8. An administrator
9. An advisor or consultant etc.
10. A CEO

In addition, we play so many roles but the primary responsibility is how we play these roles, how we handle these roles. If all the roles are played to perfection there is harmony in life. If you play your role better you can have success in your personal life, professional life, social life etc. In life, success or failure depends upon how we play these roles whatever may come next and how much time to devote to these roles. It depends on one's interested and deep-rooted efforts to succeed in those pursuits. There are 100s and 1000s of books written on time management but the best way to manage your time is to balance your roles so as to bring great harmony in your life. Each winner's profile differs from the other ; you are your best judge. Follow your heart or intellect whatever you call it. The choice is yours, do not do it by chance. Choice is governed by planning, chance is governed by destiny. Choices lead us to better human effort and better results than destiny. The destination is the same but how you reach it is very important. Luck should not determine our future. Freewill, choice, or effort has to determine our future.

ATTITUDE
IS
EVERYTHING!!

HOW MUCH DO YOU
SEE OF AN ICEBERG?

ONLY 10% OF ANY ICEBERG
IS VISIBLE.
THE REMAINING 90% IS BELOW
SEA LEVEL.

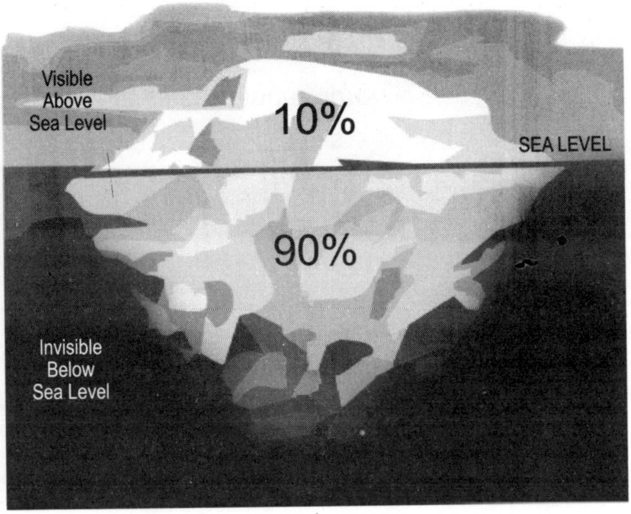

THE ICEBERG PHENOMENON IS ALSO APPLICABLE TO HUMAN BEINGS

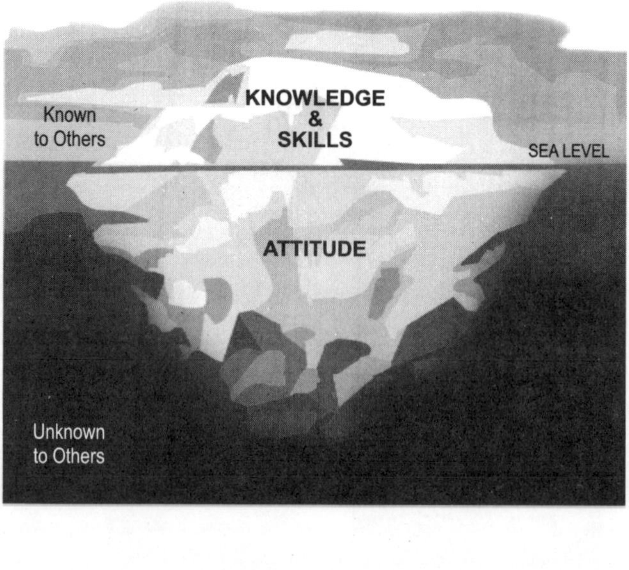

IN
OTHER WORDS

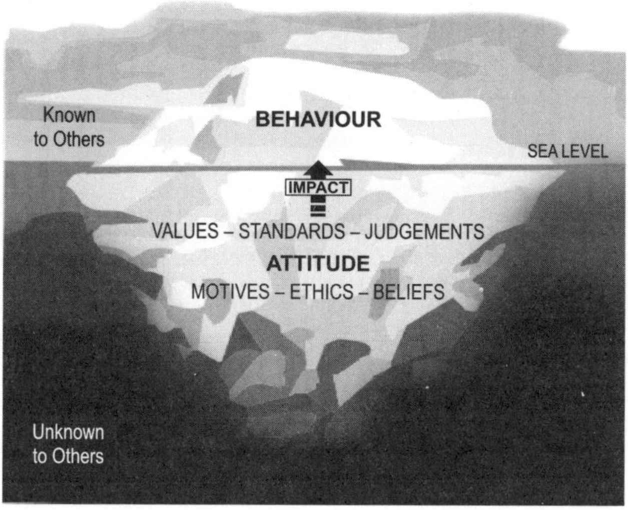

PART-II

INDIAN ETHOS IN MANAGEMENT

Fortune Favours The Brave.

–Publius Terence

3

KING OF ALL TIMES – GOOD TIMES, HARD TIMES

Communication is to respect human intellect. If I respect the human intellect, I acquire knowledge. I will go for words which convey rather than words which are meant to impress. The faculty of reasoning is available only to Man. Intellect is the faculty of reasoning in us. All other living beings are denied this faculty. For this reason alone we are superior to other beings. However, I am ashamed to tell all of you that in the past I did not care to develop my reasoning or thinking faculty. I did not realize that thinking was skilled work. On the contrary, I believed that thinking was a natural process like breathing or eating. I felt that I could think and think clearly, without any effort on my part. Today I am convinced, after my experiments in personal and official work that to develop the faculty of thinking and reasoning, I need to devote as much time and effort as I would to learning any other skilled work.

In the world today, few have developed this art of thinking. Most human beings possess groundless beliefs. His or her beliefs rest upon mere tradition or someone's bare assertion unsupported by any proof. Many of my strongest beliefs had taken root in my early childhood. I found an answer with conviction only today using my own experience and faculty of reasoning. With these facts in mind I look at the present day working in organizations. One set of people are hawking morality and principles with their own precepts. Another set is blindly accepting them without reasoning or after experimenting with them. People are affected with worries and anxieties. They undergo mental tension for what they think they are not responsible. They suffer from the strain and stress of life. They have to undergo all tests of logic. This complies with the principles of sound judgment. Those that are acceptable to our reason we should apply in our day-to-day activities. Verify their authenticity and then only come to conclusions. In addition, with this personal experience if we delve deeper into truths of reasoning, I feel we will definitely succeed.

Business schools / colleges and B-schools like IIMs, IIPM / IITs and the Harvard Business School can teach you analysis but real life needs synthesis.

People and Temperaments

There are three kinds of emotional temperaments depending upon one's mental makeup.

First Type

A self-centred man focuses all his interest and attention upon himself. His entire actions and perceptions, emotions and thoughts are directed only to the welfare of his individual benefits. However, no organization is designed to cater to any particular individual. As a result, his demands remain ever unfulfilled. His mind is never at rest. He is always discontented and disturbed. It can be brought to rest only by external agencies. (Ex. alcohol, sleeping pills etc.) Once that agency is removed, he is distracted again.

Second Type

A better-evolved or developed person possesses a stable mind. His mind does not topple over all the time. It normally remains in a stable state. However, when it is disturbed by an external agency ripples of agitation are produced in his mind. These agitations take time to subside. Consider, for instance, that one gentleman is insulted. Someone flings a nasty remark at him. This upsets his mental balance. It agitates his mind. The agitation may continue for many hours, days, or months. In certain cases, it may even prolong for years and years. Even a single disturbance can cause such havoc. The effect of the remark lingers. Such a mind is in imperfect equilibrium.

Third Type

A fully evolved or developed man is one who is very free from restless agitations of the mind and their hangover. His mind can never be disturbed. Place him in the best or worst of situations and circumstances and he is just the same. Give him joy or sorrow he is unperturbed: treat him with honour or dishonour, his mental balance is not upset.

Let us analyse which type of temperament we fall in to and change ourselves with the power of reasoning and practice.

The Bhagwat Gita is the ultimate solution to the major quests of mankind, (i.e.), the removal of sorrow and the search for the ultimate truth.

It serves the abovementioned with the message of strength, duty, and dynamic living.

The seven great management books in the world are the *Gita*, the *Ramayana* and the *Mahabharata*, the *Vedas*, *Upanishads*, the *Bible* and the *Kuran*.

The word *Veda* literally means knowledge, the knowledge par excellence or supreme knowledge par excellence. *Vedanta* is the end portion of this supreme knowledge (*Upanishads*). If the entire *Vedas* are compared to a cow,the Bhagwat Gita is the milk of that cow.

A child grows by learning from others not by

imitating them, and so does a nation, but it learns from the best. East or west, my guru is the best. Every nation has its own management ethics, based on its own unique cultural ethos...

1. The British make loyalty their management mantra
2. Performance means the most to the American
3. Japanese management theories are based on Buddhism and Confucianism
4. European management techniques run on Protestant beliefs
5. What is India's management identity?

There is a wealth of knowledge of unfathomable depth, in ancient Indian thought. The central idea in the Indian approach to management is to empower man. Machines, materials and everything else is taken care of when man is taken care of . The gist is here below. The three basic principles that guide the Indian ethos in management are

1. *Tat vam asi* - you are that (Supreme), each one of us has immense potential.
2. *Atmano mokshaya jagat hitaaya ca* - (for one's own emancipation or development and for the good of humanity
3. Subjectivity - *Sukshma* or the substitute subjective, intangible factors are more important than the *sthula* or gross, concrete, objective, tangible

factors. A manager must develop the third eye like lord Shiva's third eye of wisdom and intuition. A leader has to have vision, insight, and foresight.

The first three pursuits of *Dharma, Artha,* and *Kama* are meant for one to discover this maturity by going through experiences in life and seeing the limitations of pursuit of power, prestige, and pleasure.

There are four stages of human life .The first three stages are as student, householder and in retirement These help one to achieve the goals in life. The last stage, renunciation helps one to achieve the iultimate goal of life.

Karma Yoga

In all activities, one should get so engrossed that one should forget the work being done.

Goals in Life and Goal of Life

The four *purusharthas* (pursuits for which one must strive) of human life are

(1) *Dharma* - Good values, doing one's duty, righteousness etc for social order and a moral life

(2) *Artha* - Economic pursuits of wealth and power

(3) *Kama* - Desire fulfilment and pursuit of pleasures

(4) *Moksha* - Emancipation from the ego and discovery of one's true nature as *Atman* or Soul

Artha and *Kama* must be based on *Dharma*. *Dharma* must be given preference over *Artha* and *Artha* over *Kama*.

The verse implies four points

1. Focus on action for a process-oriented approach.
2. Do not entertain idle imagination with the results.
3. Do not insist on gaining a fixed result only.
4. Do not sit back courting inaction .Such a performer will not care for success or failure, as work itself is a joy. This is fully process oriented and not result oriented. Ensuring the best inputs in the process ensures the best results.

Past	=	Regrets + Lessons
Present	=	Feverishness + Action
Future	=	Anxiety + Planning

Through *Karma yoga,* one learns to shed regrets, feverishness and anxiety. One should learn from the past, plan for the future and act well in the present.

Achieve total quality management by total quality mind.

Vedanta is the metaphysical heritage of our

country where problems, more than being solved are dissolved.

The law of *Karma* : We get what we deserve. We do not get what we do not deserve or rather lose what we deserve. Not everybody makes it to the CEO slot.

Fear is the opposite of happiness.

Four levels of fear

1. Biological (fear of being hurt physically)
2. Emotional (losing one's possessions or relationships)
3. Intellectual (fear of failure, criticism, ideas not being accepted)
4. Spiritual (fear of the unknown)

Ignorance is the root cause of all fears. Knowledge is power and makes one fearless at all these four levels.

1. *Karma yoga* is selfless activity dedicated to a selfless cause. It is inspired action not mere work or labour. It is to love the very work at hand.
2. *Bhakthi yoga* is devotion – love directed towards the divine. The quality of thoughts improves worship of the divine, by adoring the noble ideals represented by the idols.
3. *Jnana yoga* is to turn one's attention from the seen to the seer. It is to change the direction of seeking. Until now, one was seeking happiness outside. Now one seeks it within oneself.

4. Adi Sankaracharya was one of the most well known propounders of Advaita.

Principles of Indian ethos for management

1. Infinite potential - The basic principle. Each soul is essentially divine. Discovering divinity is the purpose of work.

   i) *Tat tvam asi* - you are that (Supreme) body that can make himself a genius.

   ii) *Aham Brahmasmi* - I have immense potential. Impossible is a myth. Know that and say I am the *atman*, I am the *Brahman*, I am not this body, mind and intellect.

2. Why work?

   At mano mokshaya jagat hitaaya ca: For my personal growth, for the welfare of the world and to synchronize our personal gains with the societal benefits.

3. What is work?

   Yagnayacharatah Karma : work to be done with the spirit of *yagna* (team work, selflessness)

4. *Parasparam bharayantah:* nurture each other (win - win approach)

5. *Seva + tyag;* serve others; give your best for the good of others.

6. *Yogah karmasu koushalam;* dexterity and excellence in action is *yoga*

7. Resources: *Suskhsma* / subjective or subtle factors are more important than the objective or gross factors.

8. *Karma Kshestra* is *Dharma Khestra* making the work place clean, sacred and bringing orderliness and regularity.

4

MANAGEMENT MINDS

The manager's job is to produce performance producing results is not the manager's job; workers; are to produce results.

IEM concepts (Indian Ethos in Management)

1. Produce performers
2. Manage yourself. Be centred.
3. Mobilize men and facilitate others to readiness
4. Obtain agreement and commitment on means and ends
5. Inspire, empower, attract people
6. Set a personal example visible, accessible and on the move
7. Facilitate, show ways to overcome obstacles, participate in informal gatherings
8. Make queries, sound out ideas, and encourage suggestions

The top management's job is to envision.The manager's job is to produce performers to achieve the vision. The supervisor's job is to solve the problems of the workers. The worker's job is to produce results by executing the projects.

Our management style is more holistic. It emphasizes harmonious growth of physical, mental, intellectual, and spiritual personalities in men. It prefers the natural leader to the official leader.

Leadership is subliminally spiritual. It is transformational leadership.

Conflict Resolution

A well-known concept in the Indian tradition is the set of four methods used in dealing with situations of potential or actual conflict: *Sama, Dana, Bheda* and *Danda.* A detailed consideration of the use of the appropriate method is found in Kautilya's *Arthashastra*

Sama or Conciliation: There are six ways of adopting a conciliatory attitude

- Praising the merits, knowledge, personal qualities of someone likely to be 'inimical'.
- Mutual connections and extolling common relationships such as blood relationship, relationship by marriage, a common teacher, friends, etc.,
- Explaining the mutual advantages that will accrue to each of the two parties.

- Raising the hopes of the other by placing oneself at the other's disposal
- Establishing identity of interest.
- Giving awards and honours is a method of conciliating a potential (internal) enemy.

Dana: Placating with Gifts:

Rewarding with money, granting favours, exempting from taxes and giving employment. Gifts are of five kinds; relinquishing what is owed; continuing a payment already being made; return of something received; giving something new out of one's own wealth.

Bheda or Sowing Dissension: Sowing seeds of dissension between two enemies by creating mutual suspicion between them or by threatening one of them.

Danda or Use of Force: As a last resort, force can be used to deprive a person of his property, liberty of life (plunder, harassment, and death)

Make it a Policy

Sama - to treat equally; can be used to increase the feeling of belongingness.

Dana- to reward; can be used to acknowledge a person's contribution.

Bheda- to discriminate; can be used to focus on shortfalls of a person in critical light.

Danda- to punish; can be used to maintain discipline.

Management - 'Wise'!

Management skills practised in ancient times have merely taken on new forms or structures; whereas the underlying principles have virtually remained the same. An example is given below.

Mahabharata War Inevitable

After the exile period had terminated, Yudhishtra demanded back his kingdom of Indraprastha. The last mission of the ambassador of the Pandavas (Lord Krishna) to Dhritrashtra failed because of Duryodhana's stubbornness and war became inevitable. Dhritrashtra then sent his charioteer Sanjay to persuade Yudhishtra and Arjuna to restrain the Pandavas to get their rightful share by highlighting the evil dimensions of war. Yudhishtra was not persuaded since it meant running away from one's duty.

Fairness with Firmness

The good are often misread as being weak. Up to a certain point, goodness must be practiced, but, at times, resorting to ruthless action in a competitive market is essential. Careful planning by ascertaining the correct legal position, finding competent allies, and knowing the strengths and weaknesses of the opponents are all important. The wrong doer will project his actions as being righteous and tender advice subtly to create differences amongst the members in the opposing organization. Once deciding to take a tough stand, there should be no withdrawing until the wrong doer is suitably punished.

- Management must never negotiate out of fear but also should not fear to negotiate.
- The business environment demands fairness coupled with firmness.
- At times, in the larger interest of the organization, it is necessary for the manager to be ruthless and firm in taking decisions.

Management is meant for man to find harmony with the 'age' (era) in which he lives. The human mind being the same, ancient wisdom is very much relevant even in the modern context. Management is meant for man to 'age' (mature, evolve).

SWOT in *Panchatantra*

SWOT - Strengths, Weakness, Opportunities, Threats.

SWOT is an acronym for the internal strengths and weaknesses of business and environmental opportunities, as well as the threats faced thereby.

The stag and his antlers: Once upon a time, there lived a stag in a dense forest. One day, he went to a lake to quench his thirst. There he saw his reflection in the water and thought to himself, "I've got beautiful antlers, but my legs are ugly. I can't understand why God has given me such thin legs."

Just then, he heard a lion roaring at a short distance. The stag knew that if he stayed there, the lion would kill him. Therefore, he started running. The lion too started chasing the stag. The stag ran faster and faster and soon outdistanced the lion. Suddenly, the antlers of the stag were entangled with the overhanging branches of a tree. He thought to himself, "My thin legs helped me get away from the danger, but my antlers proved dangerous for me." By that time, the lion had reached there. He pounced upon the stag and killed him.

Moral: SWOT Analysis must be done objectively.

Strength : Strength is a resource; a skill to be in tune to meet the market demands and stand firm with competitors.

Weakness : It is a limitation or deficiency of resources, skills, capabilities, potentialities that affect effective performance.

Opportunities: One needs to grab opportunities analyzing the positive and negative sides of the coin.

Threats : They are like ticking time bombs, which are to be defused before they blast.

Over 2000 years ago, the *Thirukkural* verses reflected on SWOT

Calculate job requirements, own strength, opponent's and aids, fixing advantage before action. *(Verse no.471)*

Enthusiasm without capacity crashes one down *(Verse no.473)*

One not adjusting oneself nor aware of strength but indulgent in self praise, will be wrecked *Verse no.474)*

WHAT MAKES YOUR LIFE 100%

Let each letter of the alphabet has a value equal to its sequence of the alphabetical order:

A	B	C	D	E	F	G	H	I	J	K	L	M	N	O	P	Q	R	S	T	U	V	W	X	Y	Z
1	2	3	4	5	6	7	8	9	10	11	12	13	14	15	16	17	18	19	20	21	22	23	24	25	26

S	K	I	L	L	S
19	11	9	12	12	19

= 82

K	N	O	W	L	E	D	G	E
11	14	15	23	12	5	4	7	5

= 96

H	A	R	D		W	O	R	K
8	1	18	4		23	15	18	11

= 98

A	T	T	I	T	U	D	E
1	20	20	9	20	21	4	5

= 100

The Most Significant Change In A Person's Life Is A Change of Attitude.
Right Attitudes Produce Right Actions.

–Anonymous

5

EMPOWER AND EXCEL

Is there excellence in India? Let us examine some examples. The traditional Rajasthan carpenters have a unique work culture. If there are seven of them in a group, anyone of the seven may go to procure the order. After that, all the members of the group will sit together for discussion. They will decide how the work is to be done and who will do what. One member will design, another will purchase materials, and then another will burnish and so on. For the next order, they do not necessarily take up the same roles, instead they take turns.

These artisans and workers are egalitarian in their management; they are quality conscious; they help the juniors to develop themselves by empowering them and they work as a well-knit team with excellent team spirit.

Alternatively, take the case of the nearby grocer's

shop. He handles more than 100 items. More than 500 customers visit him daily. He knows the needs of every customer. He does not know their names, but he knows where they stay, what products they buy, whether they like Colgate or Promise. He does not know what Management Information System (MIS) is, yet he knows where his customers come from and what they want. He has his inventory and accounts. Just imagine, if a professional company has to handle so many items and customers daily, how many departments it would need! However, do we see the excellence in the grocer?

Visit Moradabad. It is famous for brassware. The workers do not know what ISO is or TQM. They do not have English-speaking managers; yet they export all their products.

One may argue that this working method may be all right for a small team. However, in a large organization, where more than 5000 people work, how is one to implement this system?

The answer is: A large organization consists of many small units (departments, divisions etc) It is possible to start a Break Through Strategy (BTS) in these small units by establishing formal supplier-customer relationship among them and gradually covering the whole organization.

6

MANAGEMENT TECHNIQUES

Techniques such as MBO, PERT, Milestone Chart and CPM are well known in industry and business. Does the Indian Ethos have any techniques akin to these? The Ashtanga Yoga of Maharishi Patanjiali provides one of the most comprehensive management techniques from the conception of a project until its successful completion.Here it is:

Eight Fold Path	Significance:	Applications in Industry
Yama	Invoking the higher force	Visioning
Niyama	Conservation of energy	Strategizing
Asana	Settling down	Resource mobilization
Pranayama	Regulating the life force	Setting up infrastructure

Pratyahara	Withdrawing the mind from distractions	Drawing the line between core and allied functions
Dharana	Retention of the mind Concentration	Building one's core competence
Dhyana	Meditation	Meeting the strategic objectives
Samadhi	Realization	Realizing the market potential

Managing by Intuition

Management without a Manager

The culmination of all management styles is to manage without a 'Manager'. Once the projection of 'I' and 'me' ceases, there is perfect management without a manager. The disappearance of ego from the enlightened manager is the acme of inner perfection - Then there is a serene silence behind dynamic activity; only then is there right action every moment without a shadow of yesterday's regrets, or tomorrow's anxieties. When we remain in the state of pure attention, leaving no room for the false ego to raise its ugly head, every decision and action gains a touch of excellence. *Vedanta* is the metaphysical heritage of our country where problems, more than being solved are dissolved. In the name of sophistication and many technical details, we generally are stressed. Transcendental Understanding can give to every manager the greatest relief, as spiritual insights lift him or her to an entirely different, higher plane. It certainly does not make him or her neglect duties, but it refreshes, revives, and rejuvenates the person.

Every manager can develop intuition through *satsang* - spiritual association, meditation, prayers, charity, selflessness and through books like the *Ramayana, Mahabharata*, the *Gita, Guru Granth Sahib*, etc.,

Until now, the predominant management approach has been a logical, analytical, 'left-brain' style. Today, a new style that blends analysis with intuition and insights is being developed, especially by Japan. More and more leaders are coping with rapid changes by sharpening their intuitive, inductive skills and values in business and management.

In a short span of five to ten years, Swami Vivekananda, Samartha Ramdas Swami, Swami Chinmayananda, Swami Shivananda established global organizations and managed them effortlessly. Think about their management skills and organizational capacities. This is management without a 'Manager'.

I Am Always Doing Things I Can't Do,
That's How I Get To Do Them.

–Pablo Picasso

7

STRESS MANAGEMENT

Do not let Stress Mess!

Be yourself. Find out your temperament and act in line with it. Imitation causes a lot of stress.

Perform duties without attachment and insistence on particular results. Accept the results gracefully, gratefully. Spend some time in doing *Pranayama.*

Follow moderation-yoga. Moderation in food, sleep, speech, exercise, recreation clubbed with meditation, eliminates stress.

There is nothing which is more purifying than knowledge. Clarity in thinking about the roles that we are playing and the essential reality that we are is important.

Faith in the Higher Reality is a great source of strength. A man is what his faith is. As our faith so will be our desires, thoughts and actions.

Just when the Mahabharata war was to begin, Arjuna, the greatest archer of his times, breaks down when he sees Bhishma, Drona and other 'relatives.' Physically he was shivering and sweating. He could not hold his bow - Gandiva. His mouth was parched. His skin was burning. He had tears in his eyes. Emotionally, he was overcome with attachment. Intellectually, he was deluded about his duty. This stress is the Arjuna-disease each one of us goes through when faced with a challenge.The Bhagavat Gita is the Krishna-cure for this disease. After listening to the *Gita,* Arjuna regained his composure and strength.

Modern psychology says that there should be "healthy stresses in life, which motivate one towards action." Indian masters say that all stress is unhealthy and one can be totally stress-free. The Sthita Prajna Lakkshana in the second chapter of the Bhagavat Gita mentions the characteristics of a person who is completely free from stress.

Time Management

"Plan out your work, Work out your plan."

The quality of your life is determined by the quality of your time spent. Time is the currency of the first century. Indian philosophical thought shared some valuable insights on time as well.

High Priority Tasks

"O Bharata, there are tasks, where the investment is small, the returns are high. Hope you identify such High Priority Tasks."

Stephen Covey calls it first things first. Never give in to urgency syndrome, neglecting what is truly important.

The most important two words for Time Management are No and Now

For action: 'Now' is the time. Never procrastinate.

For distraction: 'No' is the right word.

The Bhagavat Gita (Ch. Verse 17) says that moderation in food, sleep, action, and meditation increases one's efficiency and alertness. Fatigue and illness are major time-wasters.

The ashram system of Indian culture helps one to plan the time of one's life. Whatever be the life span, we find that this pattern of living is universally applicable in any era.

India has given to the world the smallest measure of time called *krati*. It is 000th of a second. The biggest measure of time is also given by India, called one *kalpa* - . billion years, i.e. one cycle of creation, or age of the Universe.

Indians were also the pioneers in discovering

timelessness; how to transcend the relative reality of time and space and discover infinity.

Anger Management

'A hungry man is an angry man....'
"Anger is nothing but an attachment for
An object when expressed towards an
Obstacle between ourselves and the
Object of our attachment."

Swami Chinmayananda

Anger is the root cause of adversities; it is the cause of bondage and a destroyer of righteousness. Hence, anger must be given up.

Short-term solutions:

Upadesha Saar says:

Control of the breath leads to control of the mind. The Pranayama Mantra helps one to overcome the negativities and restlessness of the mind says the *Gita*. Silence helps to control the mind. Stop speaking if you are too agitated. Observing silence helps.

Long Term Solutions

The *Gita* says:

Attachment is the root cause of fear and anger.

One who is detached becomes peaceful.

- 'Through the company of the good, one becomes detached.'
- Non-violence, truth, sacrifice, peace, and absence of crookedness and anger are the qualities of the strong and divine.
- De-condition yourself from the false thinking that an angry person is powerful, dynamic, and successful.
- As the food, so the mind. Take *sattvik* food simple, wholesome, and nutritious.
- They are in me, I am not in them. Anger is in me. I am not in it. Be a witness. Anger arises, stays, and dissolves in me.

Verses from the Bhaghavad Gita Chapter 11.62.63 trace the causes and effects of anger in eight steps as follows: Brooding over the sense objects-Attachment-> Desire-> Anger> Unfulfilled desire-Delusion-> Loss of memory-> Power of discrimination-> One perishes.

Sense Management

Control! Conserve! Concentrate!

The mind is fed and sustained, nurtured and nourished by five sense organs of perception, which draw stimuli from the outer world of sense-objects. Ordinarily we spend many of our life- energies in the field of sense - organs which are controlled, we conserve a lot of energy, as the river which is dammed, produces a lot of force.

Sense-control is a very important factor in achieving excellence. All of us know what is morally good and ethically right. However, we do not practice the same because of a lack of sense - control. The objects seem to be so enchanting that we act merely under their authority.

Some practice ways to develop sense control:

- Deny the body all that is harmful
- Oserve moderation in food, sleep and speech
- Delay impulsive gratification
- Enjoy when you are in control
- Fasting, spiritual vows, pilgrimages etc., help in developing sense control.
- Train the sense to have auspicious perception and not to seek vulgarity, obscenity.
- *Satsang* company of the good is a time-tested method for developing self-control.
- Devotion to God or a higher ideal sublimates the mental energies.
- Think! Can I get Lasting Happiness from temporary sense objects?

Sense Management can be learnt from the tortoise. The Bhagavat Gita, in Chapter II verse 5 says...

A tortoise can, even at the most distant suggestions of danger instinctively withdraw all its six limbs (four feet, a head and a tail) into itself and feel safe within.

We too must be able to consciously withdraw the limbs (5 senses and the mind)

The deer is attached to the sound of music, the elephant to the touch, the moth to the bright light, the fish to taste, and the honeybee to fragrance. These five are annihilated because of their slavery to one of the senses. What then is the condition of a man who is attached to all these five? Says Sri Adi Shankaracharya in his text *Vivekachoodamani.*

Right Thinking

As the thoughts, so the mind; as the mind, so the man. As the man, so the world.

The human mind today is completely out of control, flowing in all directions. Our primary attempt should be to prevent the flow spreading in all directions by controlling, harnessing and regulating it.

A change in thoughts can be effected by three methods:

- Reducing the quantity of thoughts
- Improving the quality of thoughts
- Giving a noble direction to the thoughts

They are declared in Hinduism by the four well known *Yogas* called the *Karma, Bhakti, Jnana* and *Raja Yogas,* respectively.

Karma Yoga is selfless activity dedicated to a selfless

cause. It is inspired action, not mere work, or labour. It is to love the very work at hand. In the absence of anxiety for results, the quantity of thoughts gets reduced.

Bhakti Yoga is devotion - Love directed towards the divine. The quality of thoughts improves through worship of the divine, by adoring the noble ideals represented by the idols.

Jnana Yoga is to turn one's attention from the seen to the seer. It is to change the direction of seeking. Until now, one was seeking happiness outside. Now, one seeks it within oneself.

Raja Yoga helps one to control the mind through the control of the body and breath

Just as the flow of water makes a river, so also the flow of thoughts in the mind. When the quality, quantity and the direction of the water in the river changes, the river is easily controlled.

These four *Yogas* prescribed in Hinduism cater to the entire cross-action of humanity. These enable:

Man to master his mind and mastery of the mind is mastery over the world. "Win the Mind. Win the World."

Energy Management

Achievements in life cannot be made by will power

alone. After having developed the will to act and achieve, one must find the energy required, within oneself. Conservation of energy can be achieved by faithfully following a way of life, subduing all agitations in the mind. Calmness, serenity and tranquillity of the mind lead to conservation of energy.

The three fundamental moral and ethical codes of behaviour: *Brahmacarya* (self-control), *Ahimsa* (non-injury) and *Satyam* (truthfulness) help in conserving physical, emotional, and intellectual energies respectively.

Brahmacarya means living a life of self-control and moderation with respect to all sense enjoyments but does not mean their total denial or mere abstinence from carnal pleasures.

Ahimsa does not mean mere 'non-killing' or 'non-injury' at the physical level. Life subsists on life. *Ahimsa* is to be understood as a mental attitude of harmlessness and love in our relationship with others in life. Not to entertain violent thoughts, ill-will about others is *ahimsa*. Even one's thought should be non -violent.

Satyam enjoins that one should live honestly with one's own intellectual convictions. Everyone has ideals, but only a few live up to them. We are led to compromise without ideals when temptations induce us. *Satyam* is intellectual honesty.

Tips to conserve energy:

Exercise for the body, meditation for the mind and study for the intellect.

- Eat fruits, raw vegetables, sprouts, dry fruits
- Deep breathing, *pranayama*, etc., help one to absorb more *prana* (Cosmic Energy)
- Chanting of mantras helps to keep mind stable
- Live in the present
- Inspiration and dedication to a higher cause
- Discover 'Truth', which is the powerhouse of all energy and dynamism

8

TEAM WORK OR YAGNA

TEAM - Together Everyone Achieves More

Yagna means sacrifice. In *Yagna* conducted in the Vedic period, the members of the community came together in a spirit of dedication and sacrifice for the purpose of a co-operative spiritual and divine endeavour to invoke the grace of the Presiding Deity for blessing the community, for the peace of the world, for prosperity etc.

In the modern context, a *yagna* means:

Any self-sacrificing work undertaken in a spirit of self-dedication, for the benefit of all.

Any social, communal, national, or personal activity into which the individual is ready to pour himself entirely in a spirit of service and dedication.

Features of a Yagna

- Driven by an inspiring goal serving the interests of everyone.
- Coming together and making the best use of the skill sets available and working with a team spirit.
- Sharing the results.

The *Yagna*-spirit is seen everywhere in nature. The sun shines, the moon appears, the sea throbs, the earth bears - all in a spirit of sacrifice and self-dedicated motherly love, never with even a trace of attachment, or any kind of self-arrogating motives.

Every sentient and insentient member of the cosmos faithfully follows the law-of-*seva* inattentively. Man alone is given the freedom to act as he likes and to the extent he disobeys this Universal law-of-sacrifice (*yagna*) to that extent he comes to suffer because of his arrogant and egoistic actions. This brings discord in the harmony of existence around him.

The *Purusha Sooktam* describes the process of creation and how the entire creation has been created through *Yagna*.

What is a Personality?

A personality is a person in reality.The physical body is the equipment with which we perceive and act. Therefore, we have to study the nature of our body and discover what is acceptable to us and what is not rather than following blindly what others say or books prescribe. You may smoke if you like or you may not smoke. However, you have to use your intellect and find out what is good and what is bad. Rely on your own experience other than on hearsay.

The mind is the equipment through which our emotions or feelings play and thought processes flow. Therefore, we have to study our mind also. (Find out the nature of your mind - love, kindness, passion, anger, hatred, envy, jealousy etc.)

Intellect is the faculty of reasoning. We discriminate between good and bad through this equipment. The intellect discriminates between cold and heat, joy and sorrow, honour and dishonour and an entire range of opposites.

The mind and the intellect constitute the inner personality. Our personality is determined by the nature of our mind and intellect. Our physical body is only a vehicle which carries our personality from place to place. It is the outer personality.

Types of Experience

There are three types of experience. They are

1. Physical Experience with our body and sense organs.

2. Emotional Experience with the mind - flow of thoughts and feelings.
3. Intellectual Experience - faculty of reasoning (intellect)

If our experiences are happy, our life will be happy. If our experiences are not happy, our life will be unhappy. When our experience flows at high frequency our life becomes dynamic. If you wish to change the nature of your experience, your attention must be directed to individual experience. Every experience is a unit of life. These units altogether constitute the whole life. Therefore, for betterment in life one has to analyze oneself, also analyze the world and mutual relationships. You also have to analyze others. One needs to know these answers beforehand if one really wants to change the activities of one's life.

If we employ these three equipments properly for contacting the world, we will gain a variety of experiences. When we contact the world three types of transactions take place.

1. Receipt of stimuli from the world.
2. Reaction within our personality.
3. Response to the world.

Take for example your present experience of reading this literature. Your eyes are taking in the stimuli in the form of letters and words. These stimuli reach your mind and intellect. A reaction sets in. It generates a particular type of feeling and judgment depending upon the quality and texture of your mind and intellect. To some, the feeling and judgment may be favourable. In that case, they will continue the study of this literature. To others the reaction may be unfavourable in which case they will respond negatively and discontinue the study.

The Acts of This Life Are The Destiny of The Next.

–Eastern Proverb

9

GUIDELINES AND PRINCIPLES

1. Avoid inflow of impure and unhealthy stimuli. They create mental agitation. They are germs which cause psychological diseases. You must examine the type of sights that your eyes see, the type of food that your tongue tastes, etc. Control and regulate the inflow of pure and healthy stimuli.
2. Having controlled the above we must also examine the reactions taking place within us, regulate, and receive only healthy stimuli. Yet they may produce unhealthy reactions like jealousy, greed, lust etc. These reactions are inevitable as they depend upon the nature of our existing mind and intellect. There are two ways of controlling reactions.This initial and temporary way is to be aware of them and check their effects from spreading further. A permanent control is achieved by channelizing

your mind and intellect. This is done by the power of reasoning or analysis and practice.

3. The third transaction of life is transmitted by your mind and intellect through the organs of action. We have to examine the quality of these actions. If the actions are selfish and self centred, they tell upon our life. They will agitate the mind. They will make us unhappy. In addition, in turn you will make others unhappy. We have to apply this knowledge in day to day living conditions (at work, office, and at conferences or at home etc.,). As I was ignorant of these facts all these years I did not know this great gift of nature. I had superiority or inferiority complexes. This can happen to any man at any level. I realized I ought not to develop such complexes. I felt that I am not any less or more important.

I have a part to play in this organization and I will do it with analysis and practice. If we make use of our talents, we can discover inner peace and happiness. No organization can cater to the whims and fancies of an individual. An organization consists of a group of individuals. Therefore, we have to change ourselves first to direct others in the right direction. This is called teamwork. Please do not accept my views blindly. Apply your own logic at reasoning and practice. Then come to a conclusion. No two individuals are alike. Everybody should view his own conviction after analysis. There is no use simply analyzing; one should understand that real life needs synthesis of all analysis.

Why Should you Work Hard?

The characteristic feature of life is motion, activity, or energy. A man or living being grows and performs all sorts of activities. A dead creature cannot produce these forms of energy. The law of evolution compels all living beings to keep moving. Any man or creature that stops activity is crushed by the wheel of time. He has to perish. There is no alternative. Sorry if I am harsh. Man's life is constant striving and struggling. Where there is no effort there is degradation and death. We must progress. It is a sin to remain static.

If a child plays with a toy, it is acceptable. However, if an adult does the same it is detestable. Again, a young man indulges in passion. It is understandable. However, if an old man does the same it is horrible. We will have to move with time. Otherwise, we will be destroyed. Man is the only being who has the faculty of reasoning or discrimination. If we use it properly, we will succeed. However, we need to first experiment and then come to a conclusion. Even a society or nation, which does not progress along with time will be ruined. Even any organization for that matter will be ruined. Even many great personalities who stopped working or who resorted to inertia met their own destruction.

Two Principles that Govern our Action

1. Attitude of Giving
2. Attitude of Taking.

If the attitude of taking prevails in an organization, you will find its staff possessed with multirole selfish demands and desires. Consequently, there will be strains and struggles only.When you switch to another company you face other problems. Problems are inevitable even in multinational organizations or in a very small company. If we change our attitude to giving, our demands will drop and desires will drop their selfishness. Harmony and happiness will prevail in an organization.

PART-III

WESTERN ETHOS IN MANAGEMENT

Do Not Wait To Strike Till The Iron Is Hot,
But Make It Hot By Striking.

–William B. Sprague

10

TRAINING, MANAGEMENT AND DEVELOPMENT

Winner's Profile

1. Any communication is effective if there is reciprocation from others. Hence, communication is to respect human intellect.
2. A person is called a professional if he has learnt the art of reciprocation for his message. Hence he or she spreads happiness through what he or she is conveying.

Now let us go into selling. It is a process of mutual satisfaction of needs or desires. The salesperson's effort in convincing and the buyer's satisfaction in getting his or her desires are a psychological, economic or social need. People also look for quality, quantity, and value for money attained or obtained. Need can arise out of mental or intellectual, physical, social or psychological desires that required being satisfied. Now the question is who has need. Obviously, Man has need but we have to sell it to the right man.

MAN means a person but

M stands for Money

A stands for Authority

N stands for Need.

Hence, we have to sell our product or service to the right man who has Money, Authority and Need. Always sell only to the right man. It is not worthwhile to promote the product to the wrong man or organization. Selling is the oldest profession in this world. Lord Krishna sold his ideas to the ignorant Arjuna, hence emerged the Bhagavat Gita. Every one is a salesperson irrespective of his profession. A lawyer has to sell his ideas to the judge to satisfy his client's needs. The judge weighs the merits and demerits of the case to decide the judgment. The company's chairman has to convince the shareholders to inspire confidence in them. A politician sells himself to win an election. For the sake of a chocolate, a child is ready to do anything. A salesperson's job begins when his customer says "No!" A superb salesman operates and fullfills either the present or the future need of his clients. He has to plan in such a way that he should make the customer want to buy his product or service. REED and ODPEC is the selling process.

Selling process

Prospecting

Now what is REED?	What is ODPEC?
R - Recognition of Need	Opening a sale
E. - Evaluation of Options	D -Developing the sale
E - Elimination of Doubts	P - Proposing a solution
D - Decision to buy a Product	E-Eliminating doubts
alternatively, Service	C - Closing of account
After sale service	Or sale

Closing a Discussion or Sale

1. Looking for closing signal
2. Effective presentation without ego
3. Understanding needs
4. Try connivance rather than confusion or corruption
5. And then win a sale.

Leadership

The definition of leadership is changing as the business world moves towards globalization, but one basic fact that remains constant is to be a good manager one must be a good leader. Good leaders have a vision i.e. they look to the future. They are human. They commit mistakes but do not commit the same mistake twice. Their work gets smarter and they develop their team for organizational success.

They are men with Reno vision (i.e.) they look at things differently, handle them perfectly and they are ambiverts.

Seven reasons for success in an organization

A- Acceptability

A - Adaptability

A - Accessibility

A - Accountability

A - Achievement

A - Advancement

A - Appreciation

How does one understand the human mind?

1. Information about his Background
2. Understanding his Physical, Mental or Social need.
3. Mutual Agreement abont his need.

Objection Handling

1. SLUSA (Stop, Listen, Understand, Soothe and

Answer)

2. Don't Argue
3. Don't Push
4. Lead
5. Concede
6. Commit
7. Convince
8. Close

Five reasons why people buy from you

Happiness

Fear is the Opposite of Happiness

Gain	- Extra Profits
	- Time Saving
	- More Production
	- Reduced Costs
Pride	- Questioning
	- Attitude for Loved One
	- Or Judgment
Imitation	- To be Good
	- Ego Satisfaction for the Loved Ones
Fear	- Loss of Life
	- Loss of Property
	- Loss of Status
	- Loss of Face
Pleasure	- For Comfort, Ease and Well being

Do not sell Logic, Arouse Feelings, or Emotions.

Make your Choice Now

Leader: Hero or Developer?

Changing times call for a change in managerial models, so say David Bradford and Allan Cohen, two top management scholars. Compared to fifty years ago, information is exploding, new areas of knowledge multiplying, technology changing, competition growing, far more swiftly, creating new challengers, and unfamiliar situations. Above all, people are more educated. In such times, the old model of the leader as one who knows best, who is always in control, who always has a better answer than his subordinates, who can pull them out of any crisis this sort of heroic model is less and less functional for it is less and less possible. For most organizations today, the heroic model is out and the new emphasis is on the manager or leader as developer.

Of course, there may be some situations today where

WINNERS' PROFILE	LOSERS' PROFILE
1. People who remain balanced in addition, clam under stress	People who permit problems to get them down
2. People who take time to teach everyone what they know	People who rush instructions to everyone and then fail to follow up.

3. People who build and maintain mutually rewarding relationships with all	Individuals insensitive to other's need
4. Individuals who learn to delegate, set reasonable and consistent authority lines score.	Those not interested in learning and those who fail to understand it is not what they can do However, what they can get others to accomplish score.
5. Winners are assertive	Losers are aggressive or dull
6. Individuals who work hard to become good communicators	individuals who let their status go to their heads
7. Leaders who build team effort to achieve heights	People who become either too authoritarian or too lax.

the heroic mode of leadership is still useful. Where technology is not changing, where the employees are not well educated, where teamwork is not crucial, there the appropriate model may still be that of the hero, and some managers may find themselves riding to the rescue in situations never dealt with in management books.

Where however, you have competent people, where their work is interdependent, where technology is changing, and competition keen and new and challenging situations a constant occurrence, there, say

Bradford and Cohen, the leadership model should be that of the manager as developer. So it is not hero, not technician, not even coach, but developer of a vision who gives meaning and inspiration to work, developer of a shared responsibility team, and developer of people, a leader under whom people grow.

Leader Developer of

1. Vision
2. Shared responsibility team
3. Abilities of subordinates

If you are Serious about Excellence

If you are serious about excellence, then you have to be serious about vision. There is no other way. People will only give of their best when they see meaning, value, significance in their work. Like the elephant in the mynah story, they need to believe. People need to believe in the work they do; need to believe that what they do matters. Commitment is a value response.

Consequently, today's leaders at every level, from CEO to section head, from principal to teacher, must provide meaning, value and inspiration to their groups. In short, they must provide vision, an exciting expression of the core purpose of the work of the group they lead. An institution must have not only a head but also a heart.

A vision is like a magnet. Steel shavings in a pile are pointed in all directions but run a magnet over them and two things happen: they are energized and they all point in the same direction. That is what a vision does; it energizes, inspires people, and gets them pointed in the same direction.

A vision is like a three dimensional picture or a hologram. What you see depends on how you look at it. Two men are breaking rocks, when asked 'What are you doing?" One: replied 'I'm breaking stones'; the other: 'I'm building a temple.' What a difference!

Leaders have to make what is of supreme importance clear and then leave room for initiative. They have to believe the vision, embody it, and voice it at every opportunity. Control comes from the vision, not from reports.

We can talk about poverty in Africa and not be moved to act; we can hear of ethnic cleansing in Bosnia and not be stirred. But when we see on television the faces of starving African children and the desperate looks of freezing Bosnian refugees, when we see the human face, the concrete human fallout of these tragedies, then we are stirred to action.

That is what a vision does; it shows us the meaning, the human fallout of our work, and stirs us to act.

If Your Actions Inspire Others To Dream More, Learn More, Do More And Become More, You Are A Leader.

–John Quincy Adams

11

MANAGERS AND LEADERS

"The manager administrates, the leader innovates.

The manager has a short-range view; the leader has a long-range perspective.

The manager asks how and when; the leader asks what and why.

The manager has his eye on the bottom line; the leader has his eye on the horizon.

The manager accepts the status quo, the leader challenges it"

—Warren Bennis

"I profoundly believe that leaders in all walks of life, whether business, politics, in the media, national or local have a role in giving an example and in articulating a vision for the people they lead and influence. They have to judge what is in others to which they will appeal. Do they appeal to the best, the noblest in the people, to their generosity and capacity for sacrifice, to their desire to be open to others? Alternatively, do they appeal to the worst in people, to their greed, their selfishness, to their fears and their prejudices? The kind of society we become in large depends on the answer."

—Cardinal Basil Hume

"Leaders provide the vision, managers carry it out, Leaders make it better, and the manager makes it run. Leaders make it happen; manager hopes it happens. Leaders create more leaders; managers create more managers."

—Bill Cecil General Author *The Five Pillars Of TQM*

"Leadership focuses on doing the right things; management focuses on doing things right. Leadership makes sure the leaders are climbing and leaning against the right wall, management makes sure we are climbing the ladders in the most efficient way possible. Most managers and executives operate within existing paradigms or ways of thinking, but leaders have the courage to bring those paradigms to the surface, identify the underlying assumptions and motivations, and challenge them by asking," Does this still hold water?"

—Stephen Covey

"Fewer things are harder to put up with than the annoyance of a good example."

—Mark Twain

How are We Doing as a Team?

"A team is a small number of people with complementary skills who are committed to a common place, performance goals and approach for which they hold themselves mutually accountable."

—J.R.Kaizenbach & D.K.Smith

One of the best ways to develop teamwork is to periodically look at how the group is working together.

Below are given twelve dimensions related to teamwork. How would you rank each of the items based on your experience?

1. Which are the areas where the teamwork seems good?
2. Which are the areas where the teamwork is not good?
3. What can be done to keep the good areas going and improve the areas in which teamwork seems to be weak?

		Always	Usually	Some Times	Seldom	Never
1.	We get all information we need for our work on time	( )	( )	( )	( )	( )
2.	Our team members participate in problem solving, decision making and setting goals	( )	( )	( )	( )	( )
3.	There is trust among the members of our team	( )	( )	( )	( )	( )
4.	Our team's work, goals and objectives are clear and challenging	( )	( )	( )	( )	( )
5.	Our team members are committed to the team's goal and objectives	( )	( )	( )	( )	( )
6.	Our meetings are effective problems are solved, and information is shared	( )	( )	( )	( )	( )
7.	The members help me when I need help	( )	( )	( )	( )	( )
8.	When we need help from other departments, we get it	( )	( )	( )	( )	( )

9.	When our team works well, it is noticed and rewarded	( )	( )	( )	( )	( )
10.	My group is moving towards becoming a self-managing team	( )	( )	( )	( )	( )
11.	I am proud to be a member of this group	( )	( )	( )	( )	( )
12.	Our group has skills and attitudes required for meeting our goals					

We Will Either Find A Way, Or Make One

–Hannibal

12

LEADER DEVELOPER OF A TEAM

The more the leader assumes responsibility for a task, the less subordinates will see it as their responsibility. Yet, as a subject, as initiator, as social, the human person needs to participate in some meaningful joint effort.

Below are methods for developing a shared responsibility team. Read them and on the next page, indicate the three methods that you feel are most required for your team.

Building a vision: The group strives to formulate an aspiring statement of the core purpose of its work.

Simply asking the group: "How are we doing as a team?" 'What do we do well?' 'Where are we weak?' Then planning accordingly.

Joint budget milking: Each section's budget is made

available to the team and a joint meeting examines each budget.

Participation in problem solving, goal setting: Together teams set goals, and work through problems.

Physical proximity: Members are close at hand; few walls and offices; co-location. Trustworthy, dear, and challenging goal. Policy of rewards goes to team as whole. Loyalty to the team and climate of trust. Open access to information; getting it to the front lines.

Pushing decisions towards one with the expertise: leader pushes influence on decision towards member with the relevant expertise.

Team members chosen for competence and collaboration skills.

Choosing a multifunctional group: All functions relative to purpose are represented; e.g., create, make, market.

"Think where man's glory most begins and ends and say my glory was I had such friends."

—William Butler Yeats

Are you Really Developing your People?

Managers can make life hell for their subordinates. Work is so important in our lives and self - understanding, that not to manage well the work of others might even be called the sin of mismanagement.

Part of the manager's function, job, and responsibility is continuous development of those under his or her leadership. Let it be said of you that under your leadership people grew.

Work should develop us. Work should not diminish us, or make us less of a person. Years ago, workers were treated as children, unequal. Today it rightly must be adult to adult. The human person is a subject, an actor, not a thing, or an object.

Furthermore, managers should develop their people not just as persons or workers, but also as managers. Today everyone has to have a managerial mind-set. Participation in planning, problem solving, and goal setting becomes more important than ever.

In fact, several surveys show that, apart from money, there are four related matters employees want but do not receive:

1. An opportunity for growth.
2. Help in planning their career
3. Honest feedback on how they are doing. Remember that even the strongest egos respond to positive feedback when it is real.
4. A boss that is open to disagreement.

To help your own efforts in developing your people, try this exercise.

Look at each one of your people:

1. What are his or her strengths?
2. Are they i.e., their strengths being used at present?
3. How could they be used? People like to do the things they are good at.
4. What training or opportunity for growth could be arranged that would help both the organization and their own careers?

Leader: Developer of People

People should grow under leadership. Some tips:

1. Learn their names. Everybody likes to be called by name.
2. Have great expectations of them. Expectations sell – fulfil. Low expectation, low performance.
3. Recognize good work. What you stroke is what you get. We all need affirmation.
4. Listen. Ask for their suggestions. Need their needs.
5. Have them participate in managing as much as possible.
6. Insist on completed stall work.

7. Being authentic yourself helps them to be authentic
8. Confront those when their performance is unacceptable, but all the while show that you value them as persons.
9. Remember you are communicating most strongly through your behaviour. Management, not speeches, is the message.
10. Be clear about what you want. Demand high standards and be relentless in pursuing them.
11. Watch your language. Avoid pejorative, sexist words, e.g., servant, fourth class; ward girl, lady doctor, and girl athlete.
12. Walk around, be visible, and develop a sense of community and belonging. Work should humanize us. People need to be involved in purposeful effort.
13. Be credible, trustworthy, and trusting. You cannot lead others if you do not have credibility. Do what you say you will do. Push responsibility down. Stick with your values and be dedicated to doing what is right.

Planning a Project?

Understanding the four basic activities involved in planning a project (planning, organizing, implementing and controlling) will increase your managerial confidence.

1. **Plan**

   (i) Review and analyse the facts of the situation. Where are we?

   (ii) Set objectives (desired results).Where do we want to go?

   (iii) Generate alternatives. How can we get there?

   (iv) What are the pros and particularly the cons of each alternative?

   (v) Decide on the basic course of action.

   (vi) Decide on the basic strategies, timings, sequence of major steps. Fix specific checkpoints to measure the progress of plan.

2. **Organize**

   (i) Identify and analyse the various job tasks required by the plan.

   (ii) Define the relationships, responsibilities, and authority of positions.

   (iii) Establish qualifications for positions,

   (iv) Allocate resources (budget, equipment, facilities)

3. **Implement/Staff**

   (i) Find qualified people for positions.

   (ii) Train personnel for responsibilities.

   (iii) Develop acceptable individual performance objectives.

(iv) Assign responsibility/accountability/authority.

(v) Coordinate on-going activities.

4. **Control**

(i) Measure plan progress against major benchmarks (Cf. lag)

(ii) Measure individual performance against performance standards.

(iii) Take corrective action on plan deviations.

(iv) Take appropriate action on individual performance (recognition, rewards, training, etc.)

Knowing Is Not Enough, We Must Apply.
Willing Is Not Enough, We Must Do.

–Johann Wolfgang von Goethe

13

THE VITAL FEW AND THE TRIVIAL MANY

The Rule of the Vital Few and the Trivial Many, or the 80/20 Principle asserts that a minority of causes, inputs, or efforts usually leads to a majority of the results, outputs, or rewards. In other words, 20 per cent of activity is responsible for 80 per cent of accomplishment in any given field

When consultant, R. Koch was a student at Oxford, his tutor downplayed the importance of lectures.

"Books can be read far faster," the tutor explained. "But never read a book from cover to cover, except for pleasure .... You can find out what the book is saying much faster than you would try reading it through. Read the conclusion, then the introduction, then the conclusion again, then dip lightly into any interesting bits,"

What he was really saying was that 80 percent of the

value of a book can be found in 20 per cent or fewer of its pages and absorbed in 20 per cent of the time most people would take to read it through.

I took this study method and extended it. At Loyola College, there is no system of continuous assessment, and the class of the degree earned depends entirely on the finals, the examinations taken at the end of the course. I discovered . . . by analyzing past examination papers, that at least 80 per cent (sometimes 100 per cent) of an examination could be well answered with knowledge from 20 per cent or fewer of the subjects that the exam was meant to cover. A student who knew an awful lot about relatively little, rather than a fair amount about a great deal could therefore much better impress the examiners. This insight enabled me to study very efficiently. Somehow without working very hard, I ended up with a First Class degree.

What is the 20 per cent of effort in my life that is leading to the 80 per cent of results?

"Eighty per cent of good management is hiring the right people. The other twenty per cent is getting out of their way."

---Score ADAMS

Getting Roles and Responsibilities Clear

You have a project. You do a job analysis and there are

many tasks to be done. Now roles and responsibilities must be made clear. For this, Beck Hard and Harris have developed a method that can be helpful.

Step 1

Write the names of persons likely to be involved across the top of the paper, the list of tasks down the left side of the paper.

Step 2

Then for each one of the tasks indicate the level of responsibility for each member of the team.

Put an R for the person who is responsible for getting it done.

Put an A-V for the person(s) who must approve or veto any decision or action involved.

Put an S for the persons who must give logistical or other support.

Put an N for the persons who must be informed of decisions.

RESPONSIBILITY CHART

Try this out with the next project. You will get much better coordination and fewer hassles down the road.

Task 1	Ravi A-V	Ghosh R	Kar S	De 1 R	Prasad 1	Menon S	Joshi A - V
Task 2							
Task 3	S	R		I		A-V	S
Task k 4	I	I	R	A-V A-V	1 S	S	1
A-V	1 S	S	1 1				
Task 5	R						

14

PLAN THE WORK AND WORK THE PLAN

Effective managers assume that, however much they plan, something is going to go wrong. There is no zero-defect plan. Discouraging? Perhaps, but they realize that when their planning is finished, their work is not done. Now they must work the plan. Plans are only good intentions unless they immediately degenerate into hard work. Now they must anticipate: Where could deviations occur because of the nature of the operation, or its time or its location or its size?

There are three types of deviations: fatal, serious, and annoying. Fatal are those that frustrate its objectives; e.g., no illumination for a one-act play contest; serious, a deviation that significantly reduces the project's success; e.g., a faulty sound system that renders much dialogue inaudible; annoying; a deviation that slightly diminishes the effect desired; e.g., a stage curtain that fails to close completely between scenes. The manager's task is to see that what goes wrong is neither fatal nor serious.

How Was I to Know?

An extra large truck carrying a vital piece of electrical machinery from Bhopal to Ranchi was forced to apply its brakes on a narrow bridge near Hazaribagh. At that, the bridge collapsed, killing several people and depositing the machinery in the riverbed.

It is not sufficient to say: 'How did we know that the truck would have to stop suddenly on that bridge?' That is the same as saying: 'How could I tell that there would be a power failure?' 'How could I know that the Chief Minister would be late?' 'How could 1 know that the forms would not be printed in time?' 'How could I know that it would rain?'

The answer is that you could not have known but you knew of the possibility and from experience knew something of the probability.

That's what management is all about; foreseeing what can be wrong, taking preventive action, and getting fall-back plans ready.

The real manager knows that plans will never go exactly as programmed. He continually thinks in terms of: "What could go wrong due to the place or the timing, or the nature of the operation itself? How serious would it be? What is the probability?

There are two types of managers: those who spend most of their time solving problems and those who spend most of their time preventing them. Try to be in the second category; there is much less competition. There is also less credit but the second type are the real managers.

Example:

Let us say you are organizing a one-act play contest among four schools. You have your detailed programme, of course, but now you must start thinking the worst. What could go wrong? How serious would it be? How probable is it? What can be done to prevent it? What contingent or back-up plans can be made ready?

Tips from a Leader

"Whenever one of my people has an idea, I ask him to lay it out in writing. I do not want anybody to sell me a plan just by the melodiousness of his voice or force of personality. You really cannot afford that.... As I had learned from McNamara, the discipline of writing something down is the first step toward making it happen. In conversation, you can get away with all kinds of vagueness and nonsense, often without even realizing it....

"Years later, 1 read Gay Talese's book on the *The New York Times*, in which one of the editors said that the most powerful position on any paper is not the editor of the editorial page, but rather the editor in charge of headlines and layout .... As the layout editor, I figured out quickly that most people do not read stories. Instead, they rely on the headlines and subheads. That means that whoever writes 'those' has a hell of a lot of influence on people's perception of the news....

"If you want to give a man credit, put it in writing. If you want to give him hell, do it on the phone....

"Now there's one phrase that I hate to see on any executive's evaluation, no matter how talented he may be, and that's the line; " He has trouble getting along with other people". . . To me, that is the kiss of death "You've just destroyed the guy, I always think." I cannot get along with people. Then he has a real problem, because that is all we have around here. No dogs, no apes —only people. In addition, if he cannot get along with his peers, what good is he to the company? As an executive, his whole function is to motivate other people. If he can't do that, he's in the wrong place."

IACOCCA, An Autobiography

TWO QUESTIONS EVERY BOSS AND SUBORDINATE SHOULD ASK EACH OTHER

1. First question: "What do you expect of me?" Research has shown:

   How greatly expectations influence our

behaviour. Expectations tend to create people in their images, i.e., tend to fulfil themselves. Take the case of a class of students and two teachers. The first teacher considers the students dull and irresponsible; the second views them as capable and mature. The performance of the students under the second teacher will be far more impressive, for she has great expectations.

How widely most employees and their bosses differ on expectations regarding their respective jobs. This bedevils their efforts to communicate and work effectively together.

By asking this question of each other, the boss and the subordinate can clarify, share, and upgrade their expectations of one another.

2. Second question: "What do I do which hinders the effectiveness of your work?"

In developing a team that runs on its own motivation and control, removing obstacles to greater effectiveness is a boss's responsibility. By asking this question, which, admittedly, requires low defensiveness, a boss generates greater understanding and receives insights they might never otherwise gain. When, in turn, the subordinates ask this question of the boss, they are perhaps more apt to listen and be drawn to a greater understanding of the key results expected of their unit.

"None goes his way alone.

All that we send into the lives of others,

Comes back into our own."

—Edwin Makkiiam

Managing by Team Objectives and Self - Control

Managing by objectives and self- control, says Peters, is still a superb tool "if the objectives .are (I) simple; (2) focused on what is important (3) genuinely created from the bottom up (the objectives are drafted by the 'living' contract, not a form- driven exercise)".

With this in mind, and with your organization's vision statement as backdrop, let us recall the steps.

1) Do the SWOT exercise: List your organization's strengths and weaknesses. Then seek the opportunities present in your present situation - today, not yesterday, — and afterwards the threats, restraints.

2) Define the long and short-range goals and strategies: Defining the business or services it is in, is a never-ending necessity for an organization. What are we trying to achieve? What is our mission, our niche, and our special contribution?

3) Key result areas: in the light of these goals, managers with their teams examine their jobs to see what the key results their teams must provide. In what areas would excellence of performance have an extraordinary impact on goal attainment? In what areas would poor performance be particularly damaging? Each manager selects three or four vital areas, the areas that determine success or failure of their team's efforts.

4) Realistic, measurable time - bound objectives are then set for each key area.

5) At regular intervals there should be a joint-objective setting interview with the superior and, if possible, team.

6) At regular intervals (three or four months) the manager meets with the boss, reports progress, and improvements, new targets are set. Therefore, it goes, not mechanically but in a 'living', flexible participative, self-managing way.

Tips for Supervisors

As the role of the manager, so also the role of the supervisor is changing. The emphasis now is on the supervisor as coach, – playing coach –, team-builder, facilitator, expediter, barrier smasher; getting things done, crossing when necessary boundaries previously held sacred; the stress on partnership, not paternalism.

The supervisor not supporting the supervisor but the supervisor supporting them. Here are some tips.

1. Know yourself

Good supervisors know themselves. They know their strong points as well as their weak points. They know where they are secure and where they will need help.

2. Know your people

Know their names. Everybody likes to be called by his or her name, Know what he or she expects, how they differ, how well the group can pull together. Know who the key people for getting group support are.

3. Know when to make decisions yourself and when to ask help from the group.

As supervisor, it is your duty to see that the necessary decisions are made, but whether you make the decision by yourself or with others is for you to decide. Shared decisions are usually best but this is not always practical.

4. Keep cool

Your men can lose their tempers but as their supervisor, you cannot lose yours.

5. Be concerned about the tasks, and even more about your people.

The best supervisor is one who is task - minded as well as people - minded. Their teams accomplish most because there have a hand in setting goals and feel they have a stake in the work, for they are treated with respect, as resources, not as cost that could be controlled.

6. Be fair

Do not play favourites. Justice is blind. Remember the hot-stove role.

7. Take responsibility; do not run away from it.

You grow as a person by taking responsibility Stand up and be counted. Be honest with yourself.

8. Foresee problems

Something will always go wrong. Foresee obstacles. Have back-up plans.

9. Develop your people

By developing teamwork, by training, by involving your people more and more in group decisions, leave your team with better people for having worked under supervision.

10. Be yourself

Do not pretend or bluff. When you say something, mean it. Remember workers take very seriously what a supervisor says to them.

11. Be a good listener

Studies the world over have shown that one of the most appreciated qualities of a supervisor is his ability to listen.

12. Develop your people

By example, by developing teamwork, by training, by involving them more and more in decisions, leave your people better persons for having worked under your supervision.

15

SEVEN WAYS TO BE HAPPIER AT WORK

1. Smile

As it turns out, smiling is directly linked to happiness. It may have started as a correlation but over time, the brain linked the two. You don't believe me? Try this: smile (a nice big smile) and attempt to think of something negative. Either you will stop smiling or you won't be able to hold the negative thought.

2. Stop worrying

Worrying happens to be one of humanity's best traits. It is the underlying emotion behind foresight, planning, and forecasting. We worry because some future event is uncertain and that feeling is a cue for us to start thinking about how to address it. The problem is, we worry too much about things that are out of our control (like the economy, stupid). The US has one of the highest rates for mental disease and yes, worry is among the leading indicators. While it's true that there are plenty of things to worry about these days, take a deep breath, America, and stop sweating the small stuff.

3. Take a break

The US is one of the most overworked industrialized nations. But this is counterproductive for a nation of "knowledge workers." Overworking people to exhaustion is a horrible way to extract knowledge from people. Taking a break provides an opportunity to reflect and often it is during such times when the best ideas, our deepest insights, emerge. I insist on taking lunches out of the office; I insist that my colleagues do the same. Call it a siesta, naptime, or a mini-vacation. It works for many of the happier nations too.

4. Do things differently

Part of the problem at work for many people is boredom. We are stuck in a rut where we come in and do the same thing over and over and over again. Get your enthusiasm back by doing things differently. Make every effort to learn, to grow, and to challenge yourself. Take on more responsibility or attempt something you never thought you were capable of doing. Even if your responsibilities don't allow for much flexibility, try a different approach to your existing responsibilities.

5. Stop managing and start leading

If you're in management, you need to find ways to motivate and stimulate your employees. How? Stretch their minds. Empower your team by giving them more responsibility, more decision-making power, more autonomy. Equally important: be inclusive. Explain what is happening in the company as a whole and give your employees a broader perspective on how their jobs influence the overall business.

6. Delegate

One of the most destructive and counterproductive byproducts of the downsizing era is fear. Many managers are scared to let go of control for fear that doing so will make them obsolete. I have news for you: if you feel that way, you already are obsolete. Being controlling is bad for business, not to mention bad for your physical and mental health. The best leaders always look for people better, smarter, and more capable than themselves.

7. Have fun

Here is some tough advice: If you don't like what you are doing, stop doing it. Life is too short to not have fun. I love what I do and when I stop loving it, I do something else. Even in this economy, you will be in high demand if you are good at what you do and can do it with a smile on your face.

Last but not the Least

Knowing the Moment

When to Talk and How to Talk

Be an Ambivert for Success in Life.

Have Balanced Mental Attitude.

Keep your Mind Open.

A parachute works only when it is open and so open up your mind.

As I felt noblest of any gift that a man can give to others is knowledge and sharing of his ideas.

When work itself is a pleasure, success or failure does not matter. A success can be a compliment to us but at the same time, it can also degrade us. A failure can be miserable but at the same time, it can also elevate us. Let us work and work alone as any work alone is a pleasure. When work alone is a pleasure, nothing can shake our personality.

Your Journey for Success Starts Now...

School for Business Leaders

Lead your Mind to Lead the World

16

SWAMI DAYANANDA SARASWATI : GUIDANCE FROM GURU

"*Namaste* or *Namaskara* is a very beautiful way of greeting each other. In every culture, there is a way of greeting. When you say *Namaste,* you are offering your salutation to Bhagavan. The person in front of you is Bhagavan!"

Greeting with Namaste

Namaste or *Namaskara* is a very beautiful way of greeting each other. In every culture, there is a way of greeting. For example, some people say "hi" and "bye". We can call this a "hi -bye culture." "Hi" you greet and "bye" you go. And there is also a shake-hand culture, in which we hold the other's hand, which is nice. "Hi-bye" is more simple and modern. When shaking hands, camaraderie and friendship are exchanged. And it also signifies "How do you do" and warmth in cold countries. In this, as we shake hands, the two become one.

Salam aleikum is also nice. With the greeting, *Salam aleikum*, you hug. This hug is wonderful; it is not just a simple South American hug. *Salam aleikum* is a little more than that and may have some additional meaning. Then we have *namaste*, which is something different. In the other forms of greetings, the two persons, the greeter and the greeted are accepted; and then the two try to express their warmth by an action. Here, in *Namaste*, the two are said to be one. I am here and you are there, still we can be friends, *Namaste is* made up of two words, *namah* and *Te. Namah* means (my) salutations, and *Te* means to you. So *Namaste* means "my salutations to you".

In yoga, there is *Surya-namaskara. Namaskara* means doing *namah* offering your salutations, your namaskara, your *Namaste*. In this word Namaste, the person is transcended, like when you say, "Touch wood" and touch the nearest wooden table. Here the transcending is not physical, because even though the table may have a table-cloth, still you touch it. You transcend the table-cloth and transcend the table to touch the wood. So when you say, "touch wood," you do not go out to touch a log of wood. Suppose one fellow says, "Thank God I was not laid off, touch wood." This is an often used American expression. One Friday passed and there was no layoff letter (pink slip) given to him. So, "Thank God I am not laid off, touch wood." That is all he said. Then I was waiting for what he was going to say next, but he went out. When he returned ten minutes later, I asked him, "Where did you go?" He replied, "I went to touch wood, because there was no wood anywhere. So in order to touch wood, I went out to touch a log of wood." No one would do this. One would touch the nearest table or chair available. One transcends the table, transcends the chair and touches wood. In fact in "touch wood," there is so much Vedanta. It takes a Swami to point it out. Sometimes they say "touch wood" and touch their own head, when nothing else is available. They transcend the head and discover what is inside the head, I think, to touch wood.

So irrespective of who the person in front of you is, still you do Namaste, and you transcend the person. Even if you know this person does not deserve your salutation, still you offer salutation. To whom? To Bhagavan, when you say Namaste, you are offering your salutation to Bhagavan. The person in front of you is Bhagavan!

The corporate language !!

"We will do it"

means

" You will do it"

"You have done a great job"

means

"More work to be given to you"

"We are working on it"

means

"We have not yet started working

on the same"

"Tomorrow first thing in the morning"

means

"Its not getting done..

At least not tomorrow !".

"After discussion we will decide - I am very open to views"

means

"I have already decided, I will tell you what to do"

"There was a slight miscommunication"

means

"We had actually lied"

"Lets call a meeting and discuss"

means

"I have no time now, will talk later"

"We can always do it"

means

"We actually cannot do the same on time"

"We are on the right track but there needs to be a slight extension of the deadline"

means

"The project is screwed up, we cannot deliver on time."

"We had slight differences of opinion"

means

"We had actually fought"

"Make a list of the work that you do and let's see how I can help you"

means

"Anyway you have to find a way out, no help from me"

"You should have told me earlier"

means

"Well even if you told me earlier that would have made hardly any difference!"

"We need to find out the real reason"

means

"Well I will tell you where your fault is"

"Well... family is important, your leave is always granted. Just ensure that the work is not affected"

means

"Well you know..."

"We are a team"

means

"I am not the only one to be blamed"

"That's actually a good question"

means

"I do not know anything about it"

"All the Best"

means

"You are in trouble"

OOO

YOU CAN HAVE IT ALL

A Simple Guide to a Joyful and Abundant Life

Arnold M. Patent

ISBN-13 : 978-93-806191-7-0
First Good Times Edition 2011

The game of life most of us are playing is not the only game even though we have convinced ourselves it is. In this game each of the players is separate, independent and usually competing in a hostile and unforgiving world. We often feel like victims.

This book describes another way of playing the game–one bases on Universal Principles–that is natural to us and awaiting our remembrance. The format of the book is a re-enactment of a typical weekend workshop during which the Principles are described and practiced.

We are not separate entities. We are all part of a singular experience: One that is loving, abundant, joyful and mutually supportive. The Universal Principles and their presentation are simple and straight forward. Give yourself the opportunity to experience this new game of life by reading *You Can Have It All.*

50 STEPS TO BUSINESS SUCCESS

Entrepreneurial Leadership In Manageable Bites

Peter M. Cleveland

ISBN-13 : 978-93-806191-1-8

First Good Times Edition 2010

50 Steps to Business Success: Entrepreneurial Leadership in Manageable Bites is a master plan for business leaders. It offers dynamic, proven techniques that will enable any entrepreneur to build a thriving enterprise.

Each step in Peter M. Cleveland's program is provided in "manageable bites," easy-to-grasp fundamental building blocks that every business leader needs. Each block is a stepping stone, guiding the reader toward effective leadership and sound business practices. From establishing a clear corporate vision and identifying concrete goals, to developing action plans and promoting leadership culture, the program details an effective strategy for business success.

With graphs and charts based on examples from real businesses, this comprehensive book offers clear, no-nonsense advice that will fit into any busy leader's lunch break or train ride home.

50 Steps to Business Success is an essential resource for any entrepreneur–whether Fortune 500 CEO or fruit stand owner.

THERE IS NOTHING YOU CANNOT BE, DO OR HAVE

RUSS MICHAEL

FROM THE AUTHOR OF LONG-TIME BESTSELLER
FINDING YOUR SOULMATE

ISBN-13 : 978-81-909396-7-6
First Good Times Edition 2010

Think about it! Is it really possible that *you* can **BE, DO** or **HAVE** *anything your heart and soul desires?*

This book will grip and hold all of your enrapt attention from **start** to **finish**! *You* will be as thrilled and enthralled--as readers all over the world have stated--to **understand** and *know* that **you** really, *really*... **can** and **will**... *materialize* your very own fondest and sweetest *dreams* on Earth.... *****You can do it!**

THE LITTLE GUIDE TO BIG CHANGES

6 Steps to Creating Lasting, Positive Change in Your Life

Sarah M. Collins

ISBN-13 : 978-93-806191-3-2

First Good Times Edition 2011

Are you satisfied with your life?
Do you feel stuck in your present circumstances?
Are you concerned about the future?
Do you feel frustrated or depressed?
Would you like to start taking control of your life right now?

The Little Guide to Big Changes shows you how to create inner changes that will manifest in the outer world.

If you're committed to transforming your life, the six techniques presented in The Little Guide to Big Changes are your answer! These are time-honored ways of making changes on the inside. If you're willing to put forth the effort, countless transformations big and small await you. As each individual's journey is unique, no two people will experience the same results. An exciting and endless voyage of self-discovery and life affirming changes can be yours when you open the door to your inner self.

Just by picking up this Little Guide and practicing what's inside, you can make sweeping changes in your own life. What are you waiting for?

THE POWER OF NEW ATTITUDE

Foreword by:
John C. Maxwell

Dr. Alan E. Nelson

ISBN-13 : 978-93-806190-6-4
First Good Times Edition 2010

When you want so much to succeed,
why are you often disappointed?

If your heart's in the right place,
why do you keep getting hurt?

You may be your own worst enemy—
without even knowing it.

Dr. Alan E. Nelson counsels people every year to help them recognize the behaviors and attitudes that defeat them. The Power of a New Attitude explores nineteen of the most common "behavitudes"— behaviors that stem from wrong attitudes—and helps you evaluate your own life to identify and change self-defeating behaviors. With this book's helpful insights, you can achieve your goals and live the successful life you long for.

www.goodtimesbooks.com

Have you enjoyed the book?

We hope this book has helped you in
Rediscovering The New World